Curls

VERSATILE, WEARABLE WRAPS
TO KNIT AT ANY GAUGE

Hunter Hammersen

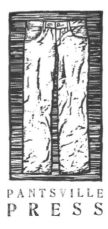

PANTSVILLE
PRESS

Charts created with StitchMastery Knitting Chart Editor.

ISBN: 978-0-9849982-5-8

Third Printing, 2015

Printed in China

Pantsville Press

Cleveland, Ohio

www.pantsvillepress.com

Contents

Introduction

It started, as these things so often do, with a swatch. A pretty little stitch pattern caught my eye, and I wondered how I might incorporate some increases while maintaining the pattern. After a bit of playing around, I found I had a rather interesting shape. A few hours later, I had a pile of swatches, a stack of scribbled charts, and (confession is good for the soul) a maniacal glint in my eye.

The more I played with the shape, the more I loved it. It was gently curved on both the top and bottom, which let it sit beautifully on all the rounder parts of the body. One or two of my swatches got wrapped around my wrists as cuffs, and some of the larger ones found themselves pressed into service as cowls. It didn't take long to realize that, if I didn't make myself stop, I'd soon have pieces that could serve as scarves or shawls.

With that, the spark was struck. I saw that I could put together a collection of incredibly flexible patterns for pieces that could be knit at any gauge, with any weight of yarn, and to any size. But what would I call them? They weren't really cowls or scarves or shawls, or at least they weren't until a knitter decided to make them so. As I looked at my swatches and admired their lovely curving forms, I realized I'd just have to call them Curls. The name seemed to fit perfectly. I confess, I'm still rather infatuated with them. I think you will be, too!

The flexibility of the shape puts you in total control. The projects shown here are made with everything from light fingering yarn to worsted weight and range in size from delicate little cowls to shawls I can wrap around myself twice. And *any* of these patterns would work in *any* of the weights of yarn and look beautiful at *any* of the sizes.

And the flexibility doesn't stop there. You can knit your Curl however you like, but you can also *wear* it in a multitude of ways. Leave the fabric open, let it wrap around your shoulders, and pin it in place (like Chlorochrous, page 62). Crumple it up a bit and drape it around your neck (like Cerise, page 17). Wrap the skinny end around the thicker end (like Pavonated, page 27). Fold it in half and pass the ends through the fold like a scarf (like Argent, page 25). Throw one end over your shoulder while the other drapes down your chest (like Caesious, page 13). Form it into a loop and wrap it around your neck (like Ianthine, page 27). Or let the bulk of the piece sit on your chest and bring the ends behind your neck (like Icterine, page 55). You really can't mess this up. Your Curls will drape beautifully no matter how you wear them. Experiment and find your favorite way!

Anatomy of a Curl

Before we dive in, let me say you can totally skip this part (though I do recommend you at least read the Hints section, page 6). It is officially allowed. You can turn to the patterns and dive right in, and everything will come out fine. That's half the fun of these projects. They just sort of work on their own! I will never know you skipped ahead, and your Curls will be lovely.

But if you do want to understand what's going on (either to modify the patterns provided here or to make up your own), this is the place to be.

I'll begin by taking you through the pieces of a Curl. Then I'll talk a bit about how a Curl comes together, how the charts are laid out, and some of the modifications you might see from one pattern to the next.

This diagram shows the five pieces of a Curl.

The pictures on the facing page show two Curls spread out flat and oriented more or less the way you'd wear them. The bound off edge (section 5) is on the bottom. The increases (section 4) are on the top.

1 **EDGE** This section makes up the straight edge on one side of the Curl. It will be two or more stitches wide and will have as many rows as the main repeat.

2 **MAIN REPEAT** This section is the main attraction. It's the pattern that makes up the field of your Curl. It can be any size.

3 **WEDGE** This section prepares you for the next instance of the main repeat. Its size and shape are the most variable of all the pieces. It will have as many rows as the main repeat, and its width will be a multiple of the width of the main repeat. It will often incorporate parts of the stitch pattern found in the main repeat.

4 **INCREASES** This section lets your Curl grow. It gives you the new stitches the wedge needs. It will be four to six stitches wide (and the stitch count may vary from row to row) and will be as tall as the main repeat.

5 **FINISH** This gets your stitches ready to bind off. Sometimes it's one row, sometimes it's several, and sometimes it's not there at all.

These five pieces, taken together, make up the most basic Curl. But if you just knit that, you'd have a tiny piece of fabric. The magic happens when you continue to repeat the edge, main repeat, wedge, and increases. Each time you repeat them, your knitting gets bigger, and it starts to form a lovely curved shape.

It all works because the wedge and the increases make room for more copies of the main repeat. That means that once you've worked through your edge, main repeat, wedge, and increases once, you've got the

3

right number of stitches to work through them again, this time with one (or more) extra repeats of the main repeat.

This is so much easier to see with a diagram. This picture shows a series of edge, main repeat, wedge, and increases worked four times. See how the number of the main repeat increases? That's how your Curl grows.

Now to keep the charts to a reasonable size (and to prevent them from looking too daunting), they'll look more like the diagram on the previous page than like the one below. That is, they'll generally only show you one set of edge, main repeat, wedge, and increases sections (plus the finish if you need it). You'll just keep working the main repeat as needed until

the Curl is the size you want. And don't worry, the colors on the charts match up with what you're seeing here, and there's always a note with all the numbers you might need. Once you've got the stitches on your needles, I think you'll find the whole process very intuitive!

Part of the fun of Curls is their flexibility. While the principles outlined above hold for all Curls, there are lots of variations. I'd like to outline a few here just so you're not surprised when you come across them in the patterns.

Each individual pattern will have a little guide like the ones shown on the next page that maps out the shape and growth of that particular Curl.

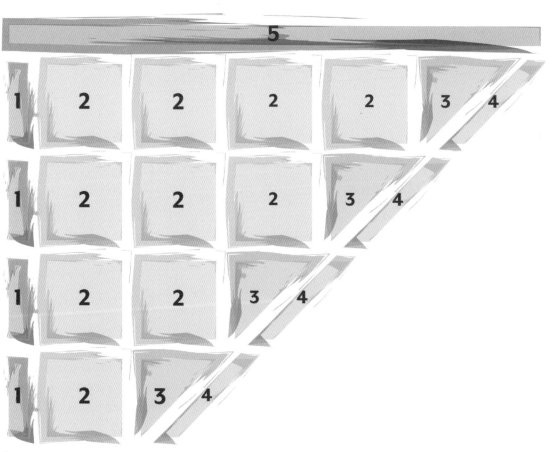

FLIP THINGS AROUND There's no reason the edge has to be on the left. It works just as well on the right. About half the patterns have the edge on the left and half on the right.

START WITH A WEDGE Often, especially if the main repeat is rather wide, there's not a good way to jump in with a main repeat right from the start. In those cases, you can start with a wedge and use it to create the space you need a little farther into the piece.

LEAVE SOME PIECES OUT Sometimes you don't need a special chart to be ready to bind off, and the pattern may not include a finish section.

CHANGE THE SLOPE In the example we started with, there was room for one more main repeat every time you worked through the series of edge, main repeat, wedge, and increases. But that isn't set in stone. You can make space for two or three or even more extra main repeats each time. It all depends on how fast the Curl grows. Different rates of increase will give you different finished proportions.

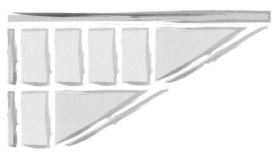

Hints

BLOCKING See page 9.

CAST ON These cast ons are quite short, so you can use whatever cast on you like best. The projects here use the long-tailed cast on.

CAST OFF The bound-off edge needs to be very stretchy, I recommend Jeny's Surprisingly Stretchy Bind Off as seen in the Fall 2009 issue of *Knitty*. You're welcome to use another, but it is important to make sure it's stretchy!

CHARTS See page 8.

GAUGE See page 7.

NEEDLES See page 7.

RIGHT-SIDE ROW Right-side rows are worked with the public side of the Curl facing you. While you knit them, read the chart from right to left and follow the right-side notations in the stitch key. See page 8 for more.

SIZING See page 7.

SLIPPED STITCHES All of the projects call for slipping stitches along the edge of the knitting to create a tidy selvage edge. There are almost as many ways to do this as there are knitters. If you're getting elongated stitches along the edge of the fabric, you're doing it right!

One approach that works for most people is to always slip the first stitch as if to purl with your yarn held to the wrong side of the fabric. If you find that's not working for the way you knit, you can also try holding the yarn to the back of the work and slipping as if to knit on right-side rows and holding the yarn to the front of the work and slipping as if to purl on wrong-side rows.

STITCH DEFINITIONS Any unusual or potentially unknown stitches are defined as you encounter them. Look for the grey boxes with each pattern for the details of that pattern's fancy stitchwork.

STITCH MARKERS You may find it helpful to separate each instance of the main repeat with a stitch marker.

SWATCHES Swatches are always a good idea. Always. That said, these projects are unusually forgiving, and getting a particular gauge isn't important (as long as you like the fabric you're getting, see page 7 for more about this). If you wanted to just start knitting and judge your fabric once you're a few inches in, I won't tell.

WINGSPAN This is the edge created by the stitches you add when you work the increases. It is opposite the bound-off edge and will likely be closest to your neck when you wear your Curl.

WRONG-SIDE ROW Wrong-side rows are worked with the private side of the Curl facing you. While you knit them, read the chart from left to right and follow the wrong-side notations in the stitch key. See page 8 for more.

YARN REQUIREMENTS Each pattern lists a generous estimate for the yarn needed to complete the project *as shown in the picture.* This is a good guideline, but estimating yardage requirements is a bit of a black art. If you decide to make your Curl with a different weight of yarn or in a different finished size, you'll need a different amount of yarn. See page 7 for more about this. Luckily, these are perfect knit-until-the-yarn-runs-out projects!

Gauge, Needles, & Sizing

One of the most marvelous things about Curls is their flexibility. You can use just about any weight of yarn, and you can make them in whatever size you'd like. That's wonderful, and it gives you a tremendous amount of freedom to create exactly what you want, but it does mean I can't tell you too much about your gauge, which needles to use, how big to make your Curl, or how much yarn you'll need.

Think about it for a moment. If I show you a Curl worn as a cowl and made with fingering-weight yarn, and you decide to knit that same Curl to wear as a shawl using a worsted-weight yarn, of course you're going to get a different gauge, use different needles, end up with a different size, and use a different number of yards of yarn. That's how it's *supposed* to work. These patterns give you the freedom to use whatever yarn you choose and to make whatever size you'd like.

I've listed the gauge for the samples shown in the book, but you don't need to worry about matching it. The most important thing to remember about gauge is that *if you're getting a fabric you like, you've got the right gauge*! If, as you work, you find you want a tighter, firmer fabric, go down a needle size. If you want a looser, drapier fabric, go up a needle size. You're in complete control.

The same applies for the size of your Curl. Have a small skein of yarn? Make a cowl. The smallest project shown here used less than 250 yards of yarn. And if you want to make a giant shawl to snuggle up in, you can do that too. You're in charge. If you're happy, it's perfect.

I do recommend checking the size of your Curl from time to time as they have been known to grow rather quickly. To do that, you're going to want to stretch it out to its full size. The edge with the live stitches wants to curve, so you need to get your stitches onto something flexible. If you're using circulars and your cable is long enough, you can use that (being careful not to let stitches pop off the ends). If not, a piece of waste yarn will do the trick. Just transfer your stitches to a piece of waste yarn, spread your Curl out flat, and see if you've got the size you like (go ahead and give it a good tug as most knitting grows a bit with blocking).

Charts

I love charts. They're a great way to present a large amount of information in a small amount of space. But as much as I love them, I realize that they can seem a bit daunting if you're not used to them. Once you get to know them though, they're really not hard. The most important thing to remember is that charts show you a stylized picture of the right side of your work. Keep that in mind, and you're halfway there!

The easiest way to get to know a chart is to work through an example. So let's talk through this sample chart step by step.

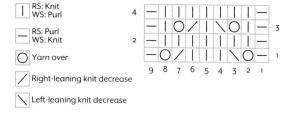

Always start with row 1, which is always the bottom row. First, figure out if row 1 is a right-side row or a wrong-side row. The instructions will tell you, but you can also tell from the chart. If it's a right-side row, the row number will be on the right of the chart. If it's a wrong-side row, the row number will be on the left of the chart.

In this example, row 1 is a right-side row.

Now start knitting! Just read across the chart and make the stitches in the order they're shown. Since you're working a right-side row, you'll work across the row from right to left and make the stitches as indicated by the right-side (RS) entries in the stitch key.

Row 1: purl 1, yarn over, work a left-leaning knit decrease, knit 3, work a right-leaning knit decrease, yarn over, purl 1.

Next, move on to row 2. All the patterns in this book are worked flat, so you'll always turn your work at the end of every row. Row 2 is a wrong-side row. Since you're working a wrong-side row, you'll work across the chart from left to right and make the stitches as indicated by the wrong-side (WS) entries in the stitch key. If a stitch only has one entry in the stitch key, it's either only worked on right-side rows, or it's the same on both right-side and wrong-side rows.

Row 2: knit 1, purl 7, knit 1.

Turn your work again, and move on to row 3, a right-side row.

Row 3: purl 1, knit 1, yarn over, work a left-leaning knit decrease, knit 1, work a right-leaning knit decrease, yarn over, knit 1, purl 1.

Turn your work again and move to row 4, a wrong-side row.

Row 4: knit 1, purl 7, and knit 1.

That's really all there is to it! Some charts are bigger, but the basic principles always hold.

The only other thing you might want to pay attention to is stitch repeats. These are indicated by heavy borders surrounding blocks of stitches. When you see these, you know you'll need to repeat the stitches within the borders as described in the stitch key and notes. You may want to separate stitch repeats with stitch markers to help you keep track of them.

Blocking

Curls pop into shape with blocking. The pieces here have all been vigorously blocked, and you'll want to do the same with yours.

Start by soaking your Curl in cool water for at least half an hour. Then, roll it up in a towel and gently squeeze out the excess water.

Next, lay it out on your blocking surface (I use blocking mats, but a bed or even a clean carpet will work) and pat it into shape.

Your shape will look something like the swatches below or the pictures on page 2 though the precise shape will change depending on which pattern you're following. The light purple swatch has the straight edge on the left. The green swatch has the straight edge on the right. The magenta swatch shows a *very* curly Curl with the straight edge on the right.

Now, pin out the straight edge. I use a ruler to keep it nice and straight. Be sure to use rust-proof pins.

Next, pin the bottom edge in a few places just to keep everything following the shape you established when you patted it out.

Then, stretch the top edge (that's your bound-off edge) and pin it in place. You can give it a good, firm tug to really open up your stitches. Depending on the pattern, the edge may have ripples (like the green swatch), or be smooth (like the magenta swatch).

Finally, remove the pins along the bottom edge as the shape will be quite well defined by the pins along the top.

Let it dry completely (I know it's hard, but it's important) before carefully unpinning.

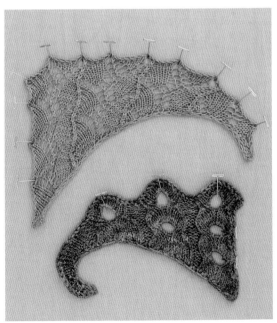

Caesious

SHOWN IN DK Weight, a DK-weight yarn by Swans Island, in the color Verdigris.

GAUGE & SIZING Shown at 12 stitches in 4 inches in pattern as charted. The piece shown used 325 yards of yarn and has a wingspan of 48 inches.

CAST ON Cast on 8 stitches.

BODY Odd rows are wrong-side rows. Even rows are right-side rows.

Work the Chart, repeating the 4 rows surrounded by the thick border as described in the key and note, until Curl reaches desired size. Each row increases the stitch count by 1. Stop after completing row 4 of the Chart.

Work a final row by slipping the first stitch as if to purl and purling to the end.

FINISHING Bind off loosely using a stretchy bind off. Weave in ends. Block to shape.

Shape

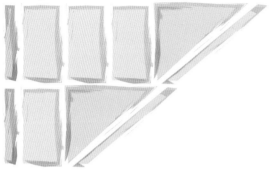

Chart

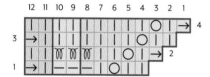

	RS: Knit WS: Purl
ͦͦ͞͞	Knit, wrapping twice
—	RS: Purl WS: Knit
→	Slip as if to purl
○	Yarn over
☐	Repeat these 4 rows until Curl reaches desired size. With each new repeat, work the yellow stitches 2 more times.

NOTE The 4 rows surrounded by the thick border are repeated to adjust the size of the Curl. The first time you work them, work the block of yellow stitches once. The second time you work them, work the block of yellow stitches three times. Each subsequent time you work them, work the block of yellow stitches two more times.

KNIT, WRAPPING TWICE Knit, wrapping the yarn around the needle twice. On the next row, when you come to this stitch, drop the extra loop of yarn off the needle.

Cerise

SHOWN IN Road to China Light, a fingering-weight yarn by The Fibre Company, in the color Rhodolite.

GAUGE & SIZING Shown at 16 stitches in 4 inches in pattern as charted. The piece shown used 425 yards of yarn and has a wingspan of 46 inches.

CAST ON Cast on 10 stitches.

BODY Odd rows are right-side rows. Even rows are wrong-side rows.

Work the Chart, repeating the 2 rows surrounded by the thick border as described in the key and note, until Curl reaches desired size. Each row increases the stitch count by 3. Stop after completing row 4 of the Chart.

Work a final row by slipping the first stitch as if to purl and knitting to the end.

FINISHING Bind off loosely using a stretchy bind off. Weave in ends. Block to shape.

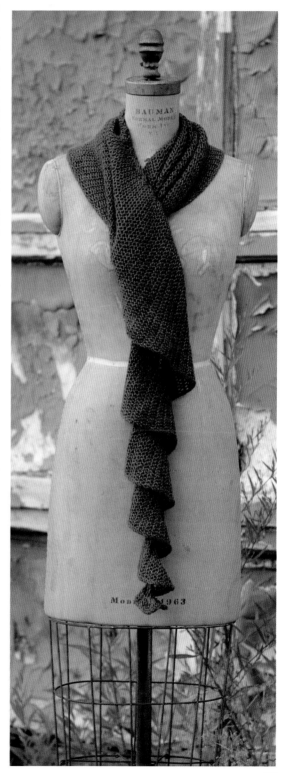

Shape

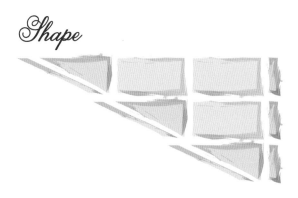

Chart

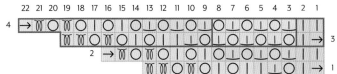

	RS: Knit
	WS: Purl

RS: Knit, wrapping twice
WS: Purl, wrapping twice

→ Slip as if to purl

◯ RS: Yarn over

RS: Slip, knit, pass slipped stitch over
WS: Slip, purl, pass slipped stitch over

Repeat these 2 rows until Curl reaches desired size. With each new repeat, work the yellow stitches 1 more time.

NOTE The 2 rows surrounded by the thick border are repeated to adjust the size of the Curl. The first time you work them, work the block of yellow stitches once. The second time you work them, work the block of yellow stitches twice. Each subsequent time you work them, work the block of yellow stitches one more time.

KNIT OR PURL, WRAPPING TWICE Knit or purl, wrapping the yarn around the needle twice. On the next row, when you come to this stitch, drop the extra loop of yarn off the needle.

SLIP, KNIT, PASS SLIPPED STITCH OVER slip 1 as if to purl with yarn in back, knit 1, pass slipped stitch over.

SLIP, PURL, PASS SLIPPED STITCH OVER slip 1 as if to purl with yarn in front, purl 1, pass slipped stitch over.

Gridelin

SHOWN IN Sonoma, a DK-weight yarn by Baah, in the color Lavender.

GAUGE & SIZING Shown at 20 stitches in 4 inches in pattern as charted. The piece shown used 350 yards of yarn and has a wingspan of 40 inches.

CAST ON Cast on 8 stitches.

BODY Odd rows are wrong-side rows. Even rows are right-side rows.

Work the Chart, repeating the 4 rows surrounded by the thick border as described in the key and note, until Curl reaches desired size. Each wrong-side row increases the stitch count by 1. Each right-side row increases the stitch count by 2. Stop after completing row 8 of the Chart.

Work the Finish Chart once. You'll repeat the 6 stitches surrounded by the purple border as needed to use up your stitches.

FINISHING Bind off loosely using a stretchy bind off. Weave in ends. Block to shape.

Shape

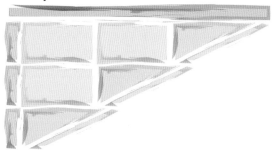

Chart

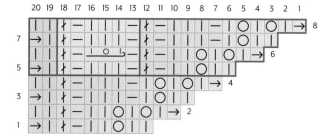

Finish Chart

	RS: Knit WS: Purl
⟋	RS: Knit through the back loop WS: Purl through the back loop
—	RS: Purl WS: Knit
◯	Yarn over
→	Slip as if to purl
I ◯ Ь	Three stitch cluster
☐	Repeat these 4 rows until Curl reaches desired size. With each new repeat, work the yellow stitches 1 more time.
☐	Repeat these 6 stitches as needed.

NOTE The 4 rows surrounded by the thick border are repeated to adjust the size of the Curl. The first time you work them, work the block of yellow stitches once. The second time you work them, work the block of yellow stitches twice. Each subsequent time you work them, work the block of yellow stitches one more time.

THREE STITCH CLUSTER Use your right needle to pick up the third stitch on your left needle and lift it up, over the first two stitches, and off the needle. Knit 1, yarn over, knit 1.

Argent

SHOWN IN Cloud, a light-fingering-weight yarn by Anzula, in the color Seaside.

GAUGE & SIZING Shown at 16 stitches in 4 inches in pattern as charted. The piece shown used 500 yards of yarn and has a wingspan of 66 inches.

CAST ON Cast on 16 stitches.

BODY Odd rows are wrong-side rows. Even rows are right-side rows.

Work the Chart, repeating the 12 rows surrounded by the thick border as described in the key and note, until Curl reaches desired size. Each wrong-side row increases the stitch count by 1. Each right-side row increases the stitch count by 2. Stop after completing row 12 of the Chart

Work a final row by slipping the first stitch as if to purl and purling to the end.

FINISHING Bind off loosely using a stretchy bind off. Weave in ends. Block to shape.

Shape

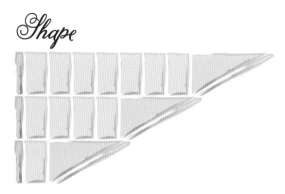

Chart

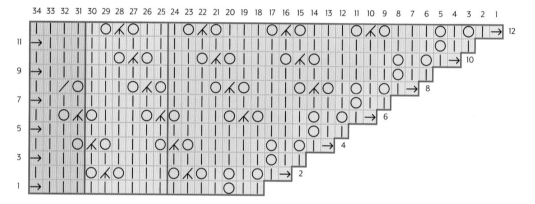

	RS: Knit WS: Purl
/	Right-leaning knit decrease
⋏	Right-leaning double knit decrease
O	Yarn over
→	Slip as if to purl
▢	Repeat these 12 rows until Curl reaches desired size. With each new repeat, work the yellow stitches 3 more times.

NOTE The 12 rows surrounded by the thick border are repeated to adjust the size of the Curl. The first time you work them, work the block of yellow stitches once. The second time you work them, work the block of yellow stitches four times. Each subsequent time you work them, work the block of yellow stitches three more times.

RIGHT-LEANING DOUBLE KNIT DECREASE Knit 3 together (similar to knitting 2 together, just go into an extra stitch).

24

Pavonated

SHOWN IN Civility Sport, a sport-weight yarn by Elemental Affects, in the color Serge.

GAUGE & SIZING Shown at 16 stitches in 4 inches in pattern as charted. The piece shown used 400 yards of yarn and has a wingspan of 44 inches.

CAST ON Cast on 10 stitches.

BODY Odd rows are right-side rows. Even rows are wrong-side rows.

Work the Chart, repeating the 8 rows surrounded by the thick border as described in the key and note, until Curl reaches desired size. Each right-side row increases the stitch count by 1. Each wrong-side row increases the stitch count by 2. Stop after completing row 12 or 16 of the Chart.

Work a final row by slipping the first stitch as if to purl and knitting to the end.

FINISHING Bind off loosely using a stretchy bind off. Weave in ends. Block to shape.

I	RS: Knit / WS: Purl
—	RS: Purl / WS: Knit
→	Slip as if to purl
O	Yarn over
/	Right-leaning knit decrease
⋏	Right-leaning double knit decrease
⋋	Left-leaning double knit decrease
☐	Repeat these 8 rows until Curl reaches desired size. With each new repeat, work the yellow stitches 1 more time.

Shape

NOTE The 8 rows surrounded by the thick border are repeated to adjust the size of the Curl. The first time you work them, work the block of yellow stitches once. The second time you work them, work the block of yellow stitches twice. Each subsequent time you work them, work the block of yellow stitches one more time.

This stitch looks lovely on either side. The pictures show both sides of the finished piece.

RIGHT-LEANING DOUBLE KNIT DECREASE Slip 1 knitwise. Slip another knitwise. Return slipped stitches to the left needle. Insert the right needle from the right to the left into the back loops of both stitches. Knit both together. Put the resulting stitch back on the left needle. Pass the second stitch on the left needle over the first. Slip the first stitch back to the right needle.

LEFT-LEANING DOUBLE KNIT DECREASE Slip 1 knitwise. Knit 2 together. Pass slipped stitch over.

Chart

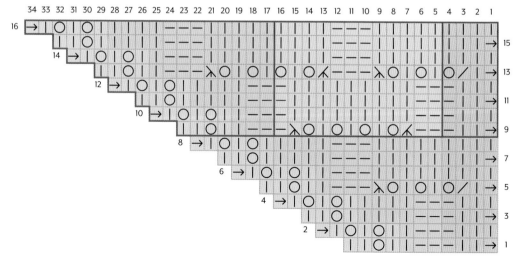

Infuscate

SHOWN IN Selku, a sport-weight yarn by String Theory, in the color Vert.

GAUGE & SIZING Shown at 22 stitches in 4 inches in pattern as charted. The piece shown used 650 yards of yarn and has a wingspan of 56 inches.

CAST ON Cast on 8 stitches.

BODY Odd rows are wrong-side rows. Even rows are right-side rows.

Work the Chart, repeating 8 the rows surrounded by the thick border as described in the key and note, until Curl reaches desired size. Each row (except 8 and 16) increases the stitch count by 2 (stitch counts differ on rows 9, 10, & 11; do not count stitches on those rows). Stop after completing row 16 of the Chart.

FINISHING Bind off loosely using a stretchy bind off. Weave in ends. Block to shape.

NOTE The 8 rows surrounded by the thick border are repeated to adjust the size of the Curl. The first time you work them, work the block of yellow stitches once. The second time you work them, work the block of yellow stitches two times. Each subsequent time you work them, work the block of yellow stitches one more time.

YARN OVER You'll notice that two yarn overs happen right next to each other. Just do exactly what the chart says, work two yarn overs in a row. You'll deal with it when you make the large increase on the next row.

LARGE INCREASE Slip 1 loop of the double yarn over off to free up extra yarn. (Purl 1, knit 1) 4 times into the remaining loop.

RIGHT-LEANING TWISTED KNIT DECREASE Slip 1 as if to purl. Remount the next stitch so it is rotated 180 degrees (one half turn) clockwise. Return the slipped stitch to the left needle. Knit 2 together.

RIGHT-LEANING TWISTED PURL DECREASE Slip 1 knitwise. Slip another knitwise. Return the slipped stitches to the left needle. Purl 2 together.

LEFT-LEANING TWISTED KNIT DECREASE Insert the right needle from the right to the left into the back loops of 2 stitches. Knit them both together.

LEFT-LEANING TWISTED PURL DECREASE Purl 2 together through the back loops.

Shape

Chart

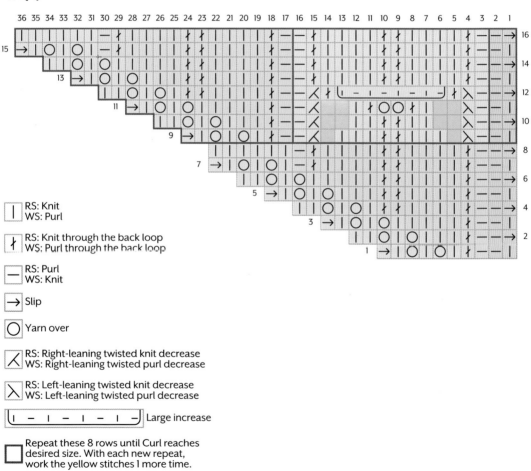

	RS: Knit WS: Purl
⟨	RS: Knit through the back loop WS: Purl through the back loop
—	RS: Purl WS: Knit
→	Slip
O	Yarn over
⟋	RS: Right-leaning twisted knit decrease WS: Right-leaning twisted purl decrease
⟍	RS: Left-leaning twisted knit decrease WS: Left-leaning twisted purl decrease
⌊I – I – I – I –⌋	Large increase
☐	Repeat these 8 rows until Curl reaches desired size. With each new repeat, work the yellow stitches 1 more time.
▦	No stitch

32

Ianthine

SHOWN IN Oriana 8-Ply, a fingering-weight yarn by Space Cadet Creations, in the color Plume.

GAUGE & SIZING Shown at 16 stitches in 4 inches in pattern as charted. The piece shown used 400 yards of yarn and has a wingspan of 54 inches.

CAST ON Cast on 9 stitches.

BODY Odd rows are wrong-side rows. Even rows are right-side rows.

Work the Chart, repeating the 12 rows surrounded by the thick border as described in the key and note, until Curl reaches desired size. Each row increases the stitch count by 1 (except for rows 12 and 24 which increase the stitch count by 2). Stop after completing row 18 or 24 of the Chart.

Work a final row by slipping the first stitch as if to purl and purling to the end.

FINISHING Bind off loosely using a stretchy bind off. Weave in ends. Block to shape.

Shape

Chart

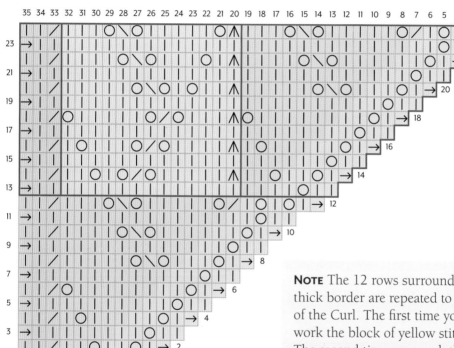

NOTE The 12 rows surrounded by the thick border are repeated to adjust the size of the Curl. The first time you work them, work the block of yellow stitches once. The second time you work them, work the block of yellow stitches two times. Each subsequent time you work them, work the block of yellow stitches one more time.

CENTERED DOUBLE KNIT DECREASE Slip 2 together at the same time as if to knit 2 together. Knit 1. Pass the slipped stitches over.

Watchet

SHOWN IN Fingering 55, a fingering-weight yarn by Claudia Hand Painted Yarns, in the color Deep Blue.

GAUGE & SIZING Shown at 20 stitches in 4 inches in pattern as charted. The piece shown used 325 yards of yarn and has a wingspan of 48 inches.

CAST ON Cast on 8 stitches.

BODY Odd rows are wrong-side rows. Even rows are right-side rows.

Work the Chart, repeating the 14 rows surrounded by the thick border as described in the key and note, until Curl reaches desired size. Each row increases the stitch count by 1. Stop after completing row 21 or 28 of the Chart.

Work a final row by slipping the first stitch as if to purl and knitting (if you stopped after row 21) or purling (if you stopped after row 28) to the end.

FINISHING Bind off loosely using a stretchy bind off. Weave in ends. Block to shape.

Shape

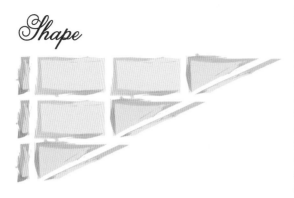

NOTE The 14 rows surrounded by the thick border are repeated to adjust the size of the Curl. The first time you work them, work the block of yellow stitches once. The second time you work them, work the block of yellow stitches twice. Each subsequent time you work them, work the block of yellow stitches one more time.

CAST ON 1 Cast on 1 stitch (I recommend the knitted or backward loop cast on).

RIGHT-LEANING PURL DECREASE Purl 2 together.

LEFT-LEANING PURL DECREASE Slip 1 knit-wise. Slip another 1 knitwise. Return slipped stitches to the left needle. Purl 2 together through the back loops.

Chart

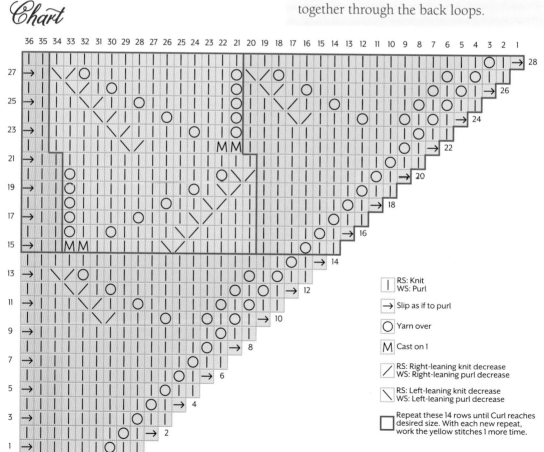

	RS: Knit WS: Purl
→	Slip as if to purl
O	Yarn over
M	Cast on 1
╱	RS: Right-leaning knit decrease WS: Right-leaning purl decrease
╲	RS: Left-leaning knit decrease WS: Left-leaning purl decrease
☐	Repeat these 14 rows until Curl reaches desired size. With each new repeat, work the yellow stitches 1 more time.

Nacarat

SHOWN IN Fourth of July, a worsted-weight yarn by Briar Rose, in a custom color.

GAUGE & SIZING Shown at 16 stitches in 4 inches in pattern as charted. The piece shown used 400 yards of yarn and has a wingspan of 44 inches.

Shape

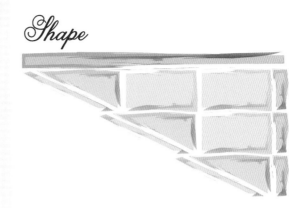

CAST ON Cast on 8 stitches.

BODY Odd rows are right-side rows. Even rows are wrong-side rows.

Work the Chart, repeating the 10 rows surrounded by the thick border as described in the key and note, until Curl reaches desired size. Each row increases the stitch count by 2.

Work the Finish Chart once. You'll repeat the 20 stitches surrounded by the purple border as needed to use up your stitches.

FINISHING Bind off loosely using a stretchy bind off. Weave in ends. Block to shape.

NOTE The 10 rows surrounded by the thick border are repeated to adjust the size of the Curl. The first time you work them, work the block of yellow stitches once. The second time you work them, work the block of yellow stitches twice. Each subsequent time you work them, work the block of yellow stitches one more time.

RIGHT-LEANING PURL DECREASE Purl 2 together.

LEFT-LEANING PURL DECREASE Slip 1 knitwise. Slip another 1 knitwise. Return slipped stitches to the left needle. Purl 2 together through the back loops.

CENTERED DOUBLE KNIT DECREASE Slip 2 together at the same time as if to knit 2 together. Knit 1. Pass the slipped stitches over.

Chart

Finish Chart

| | RS: Knit |
| | WS: Purl |

| ↑ | Slip as if to purl |

| O | Yarn over |

| / | RS: Right-leaning knit decrease |
| | WS: Right-leaning purl decrease |

| \ | RS: Left-leaning knit decrease |
| | WS: Left-leaning purl decrease |

| ⋀ | Centered double knit decrease |

| ☐ | Repeat these 10 rows until Curl reaches desired size. With each new repeat, work the yellow stitches 1 more time. |

| ☐ | Repeat these 20 stitches as needed. |

Sinopia

SHOWN IN Alpaca Silk, a sport-weight yarn by Blue Sky Alpacas, in the color Crabapple.

GAUGE & SIZING Shown at 20 stitches in 4 inches in pattern as charted. The piece shown used 250 yards of yarn and has a wingspan of 35 inches.

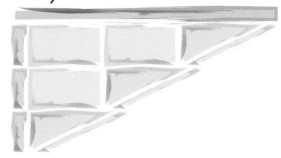

Shape

CAST ON Cast on 8 stitches.

BODY Odd rows are wrong-side rows. Even rows are right-side rows.

Work the Chart, repeating the 12 rows surrounded by the thick border as described in the key and note, until Curl reaches desired size. Each row (except 12 and 24) increases the stitch count by 2. Stop after completing row 24 of the Chart.

Work the Finish Chart once. You'll repeat the 22 stitches surrounded by the purple border as needed to use up your stitches.

FINISHING Bind off loosely using a stretchy bind off. Weave in ends. Block to shape.

NOTE The 12 rows surrounded by the thick border are repeated to adjust the size of the Curl. The first time you work them, work the block of yellow stitches once. The second time you work them, work the block of yellow stitches twice. Each subsequent time you work them, work the block of yellow stitches one more time.

RIGHT-LEANING TWISTED KNIT DECREASE Slip 1 as if to purl. Remount the next stitch so it is rotated 180 degrees (one half turn) clockwise. Return the slipped stitch to the left needle. Knit 2 together.

LEFT-LEANING TWISTED KNIT DECREASE Insert the right needle from the right to the left into the back loops of 2 stitches. Knit them together.

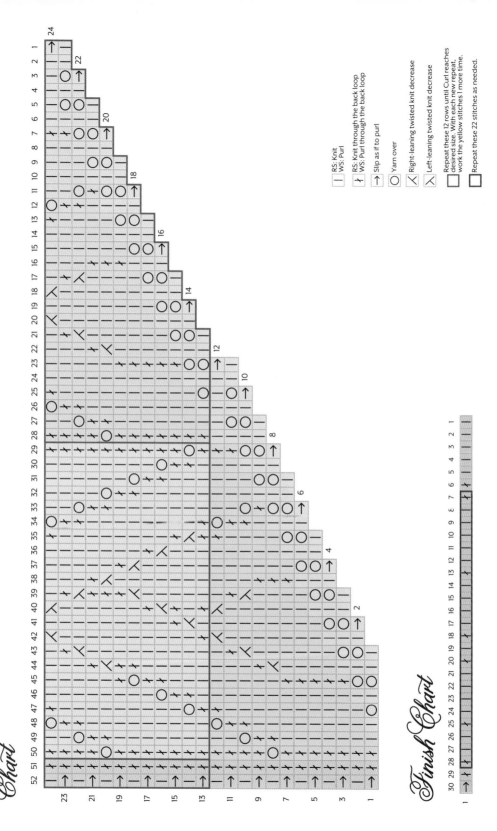

Chart

Finish Chart

Legend:
- RS: Knit / WS: Purl
- RS: Knit through the back loop / WS: Purl through the back loop
- Slip as if to purl
- Yarn over
- Right-leaning twisted knit decrease
- Left-leaning twisted knit decrease
- Repeat these 12 rows until Curl reaches desired size. With each new repeat, work the yellow stitches 1 more time.
- Repeat these 22 stitches as needed.

48

Filemot

SHOWN IN Fine, a fingering-weight yarn by Spud & Chloë, in the color 7814.

GAUGE & SIZING Shown at 28 stitches in 4 inches in pattern as charted. The piece shown used 475 yards of yarn and has a wingspan of 48 inches.

Shape

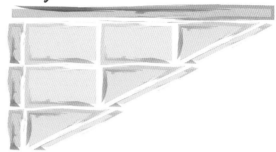

CAST ON Cast on 8 stitches.

BODY Odd rows are right-side rows. Even rows are wrong-side rows.

Work the Chart, repeating the 12 rows surrounded by the thick border as described in the key and note, until Curl reaches desired size. Each row increases the stitch count by 2. Stop after completing row 18 or 24 of the Chart.

Work the Finish Chart once. You'll repeat the 24 stitches surrounded by the purple border as needed to use up your stitches.

FINISHING Bind off loosely using a stretchy bind off. Weave in ends. Block to shape.

RIGHT-LEANING TWISTED KNIT DECREASE Slip 1 as if to purl. Remount the next stitch so it is rotated 180 degrees (one half turn) clockwise. Return the slipped stitch to the left needle. Knit 2 together.

RIGHT-LEANING TWISTED PURL DECREASE Slip 1 knitwise. Slip another knitwise. Return the slipped stitches to the left needle. Purl 2 together.

LEFT-LEANING TWISTED KNIT DECREASE Insert the right needle from the right to the left into the back loops of 2 stitches. Knit them together.

LEFT-LEANING TWISTED PURL DECREASE Purl 2 together through the back loops.

CENTERED TWISTED DOUBLE KNIT Slip 1 as if to purl. Remount the next stitch so it is rotated 180 degrees (one half turn) clockwise. Return the slipped stitch to the left needle. Slip 2 together at the same time as if to knit 2 together. Knit 1. Pass the slipped stitches over.

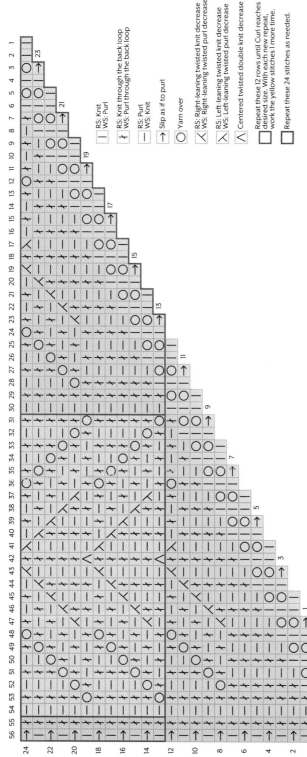

Chart

Legend

	RS: Knit / WS: Purl
⏀	RS: Knit through the back loop / WS: Purl through the back loop
—	RS: Purl / WS: Knit
↑	Slip as if to purl
○	Yarn over
✕	RS: Right-leaning twisted knit decrease / WS: Right-leaning twisted purl decrease
╲	RS: Left-leaning twisted knit decrease / WS: Left-leaning twisted purl decrease
⋀	Centered twisted double knit decrease
☐	Repeat these 12 rows until Curl reaches desired size. With each new repeat, work the yellow stitches 1 more time.
☐	Repeat these 24 stitches as needed.

NOTE The 12 rows surrounded by the thick border are repeated to adjust the size of the Curl. The first time you work them, work the block of yellow stitches once. The second time you work them, work the block of yellow stitches twice. Each subsequent time you work them, work the block of yellow stitches one more time.

Finish Chart

52

Icterine

SHOWN IN Bugga, a sport-weight yarn by Cephalopod Yarns, in the color Chester Cricket.

GAUGE & SIZING Shown at 28 stitches in 4 inches in pattern as charted. The piece shown used 500 yards of yarn and has a wingspan of 56 inches.

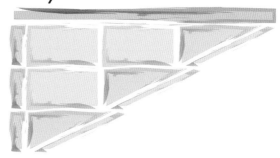

Shape

CAST ON Cast on 7 stitches.

BODY Odd rows are wrong-side rows. Even rows are right-side rows.

Work the Chart, repeating the 12 rows surrounded by the thick border as described in the key and note, until Curl reaches desired size. Each row increases the stitch count by 2. Stop after completing row 24 of the Chart.

Work the Finish Chart once. You'll repeat the 24 stitches surrounded by the purple border as needed to use up your stitches.

FINISHING Bind off loosely using a stretchy bind off. Weave in ends. Block to shape.

NOTE The 12 rows surrounded by the thick border are repeated to adjust the size of the Curl. The first time you work them, work the block of yellow stitches once. The second time you work them, work the block of yellow stitches twice. Each subsequent time you work them, work the block of yellow stitches one more time.

5X5 CABLE LEFT Slip 5 to cable needle, hold in front, knit 5, knit 5 from cable needle.

8X8 CABLE RIGHT Slip 8 to cable needle, hold in back, knit 8, knit 8 from cable needle.

8X8 CABLE LEFT Slip 8 to cable needle, hold in front, knit 8, knit 8 from cable needle.

Chart

Finish Chart

	RS: Knit WS: Purl
	RS: Purl WS: Knit
O	Yarn over
→	Slip as if to purl

5x5 Cable left

8x8 Cable right

8x8 Cable left

Repeat these 12 rows until Curl reaches desired size. With each new repeat, work the yellow stitches 1 more time.

Repeat these 24 stitches as needed.

Fulvous

SHOWN IN Bello Worsted, a worsted-weight yarn by Plucky Knitter, in the color Belgian Wit.

GAUGE & SIZING Shown at 20 stitches in 4 inches in stockinette. The piece shown used 350 yards of yarn and has a wingspan of 36 inches.

Shape

CAST ON Cast on 10 stitches.

BODY Odd rows are wrong-side rows. Even rows are right-side rows.

Work the Chart, repeating the 12 rows surrounded by the thick border as described in the key and note, until Curl reaches desired size. Stop after completing row 24 of the Chart.

Work the Finish Chart once. You'll repeat the stitches surrounded by the purple border as needed to use up your stitches.

FINISHING Bind off loosely using a stretchy bind off. Weave in ends. Block to shape.

NOTE The 12 rows surrounded by the thick border are repeated to adjust the size of the Curl. The first time you work them, work the block of yellow stitches once. The second time you work them, work the block of yellow stitches twice. Each subsequent time you work them, work the block of yellow stitches one more time.

1X1 CABLE LEFT TWISTED Slip 1 to cable needle, hold in front, knit 1 through the back loop, knit 1 through the back loop from cable needle.

1X1 CABLE RIGHT TWISTED Slip 1 to cable needle, hold in back, knit 1 through the back loop, knit 1 through the back loop from cable needle.

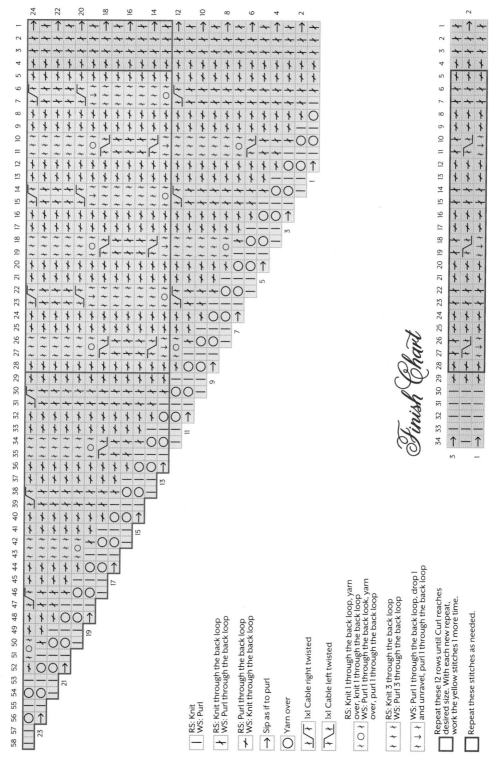

Chart

Finish Chart

RS: Knit
WS: Purl

RS: Knit through the back loop
WS: Purl through the back loop

RS: Purl through the back loop
WS: Knit through the back loop

Slp as if to purl

Yarn over

1x1 Cable right twisted

1x1 Cable left twisted

RS: Knit 1 through the back loop, yarn
over, knit 1 through the back loop
WS: Purl 1 through the back look, yarn
over, purl 1 through the back loop

RS: Knit 3 through the back loop
WS: Purl 3 through the back loop

WS: Purl 1 through the back loop, drop 1
and unravel, purl 1 through the back loop

Repeat these 12 rows until Curl reaches
desired size. With each new repeat,
work the yellow stitches 1 more time.

Repeat these stitches as needed.

60

Chlorochrous

SHOWN IN Staccato, a fingering-weight yarn, and Silk Cloud, a lace-weight yarn, both by Shibui, in the color Lime.

GAUGE & SIZING Shown at 22 stitches in 4 inches in pattern as charted. The piece shown used 325 yards of Staccato and 80 yards of Silk Cloud and has a wingspan of 42 inches.

Shape

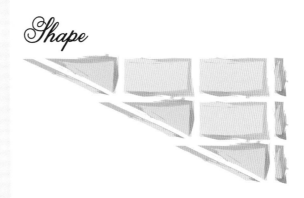

NOTE Staccato is the main yarn. Silk Cloud is the accent yarn. You will need about one fourth as many yards of the accent yarn as of the main yarn.

CAST ON With main yarn, cast on 8 stitches.

BODY Odd rows are wrong-side rows. Even rows are right-side rows.

Work the Chart, repeating the 16 rows surrounded by the thick border as described in the key and note, until Curl reaches desired size. Each wrong-side row increases the stitch count by 1. Each right-side row increases the stitch count by 2. Stop after completing row 20, 24, 28, or 32 of the Chart.

When you work rows 6, 10, 14, 18, 22, 26, and 30, use both yarns held together. These rows are marked with an asterisk on the Chart to help you remember to use both yarns. Just pick up the accent yarn, hold it along side the main yarn, and work the stitches as shown. When the row is finished, break the accent yarn and keep working with the main yarn.

Work a final row by slipping the first stitch as if to purl and purling to the end.

FINISHING Bind off loosely using a stretchy bind off. Weave in ends. Block to shape. Trim the loose ends of Silk Cloud close to the body of the Curl (don't worry, they won't come undone).

NOTE The 16 rows surrounded by the thick border are repeated to adjust the size of the Curl. The first time you work them, work the block of yellow stitches once. The second time you work them, work the block of yellow stitches twice. Each subsequent time you work them, work the block of yellow stitches one more time.

SLIP 5 STITCHES Slip 5 stitches as if to purl with both yarns held to the front (public side) of the Curl.

DIPPED STITCH Bring your right needle up under the slipped strands from 2 rows ago. Knit the next stitch. Use your left needle to pass the slipped strands over the stitch you just knit and off your needle

Chart

64

RS: Knit
WS: Purl

↑ Slip as if to purl

○ Yarn over

→ Dipped stich

— Slip 5 stitches with both yarns in front

Repeat these 16 rows until Curl reaches desired size. With each new repeat, work the yellow stitches 1 more time.

Thanks

Nobody writes a book alone. Anyone who tries to tell you differently is forgetting some of the things that happened along the way. I owe debts of gratitude to an awful lot of folks, not least of all to those of you who make room for my books on your shelves and my projects in your knitting bags. Thank you. Without you, I wouldn't be able to do this odd and marvelous thing I find myself doing!

I must also thank Laura Lazarites for her enthusiasm when the idea for this book first took hold (not to mention her lovely sample knitting). There was an afternoon or two of fervid texting during which she never once said I was nuts or told me to be quiet. She may, in fact, have suggested I wasn't all that crazy and hinted that I should stop texting and start writing. Lana Holden played a similar role at a slightly later point in the process by reminding me (repeatedly) that simple can be good and keeping me from succumbing to my natural tendency to overcomplicate things.

The members of Cat Bordhi's Visionary Authors group also provided much appreciated help and encouragement. Special thanks are due to Ann Budd, Deb Robson, Jill Wolcott, and Jeane deCoster for encouraging, cajoling, and coercing me in just the right proportions. And I would be remiss if I did not mention JC Briar. JC said yes to an astonishing number of my harebrained schemes, gently pointed out several of my more glaring errors, and just generally made writing this book much more fun.

Heather Ordover and Cathy Scott are two of the very nicest geniuses you'll ever meet, and they have both been kind enough to let me take shameless advantage of their skills. Heather looks after my prose, and Cathy sorts out my patterns. If you haven't thrown this book across the room in frustration, it's likely due to their good work.

Antonia Markiet and Jennifer Leigh offered their expert eyes and gentle advice in a moment of wavering resolve, and for that I am most grateful.

And, as always, many thanks to my family, especially my husband Brian. He wrote me a magical knitting calculator, engaged in nearly endless discussions of hyphens and punctuation, and spent an alarming number of weekend mornings in a weedy vacant lot while I took pictures of knitting. I'm not quite sure what I did to deserve him, but I'm awfully glad I did it.

Sources

Feel free to substitute yarns. Just be aware that, if you use a different weight of yarn or make your Curl a different size, you will almost certainly need a different amount of yarn.

Charts were created with StitchMastery Knitting Chart Editor.
STITCHMASTERY.COM

Caesious uses about 325 yards of DK Weight by Swans Island. DK weight, 100% merino
SWANSISLANDCOMPANY.COM

Cerise uses about 425 yards of Road to China Light by The Fibre Company. Sport weight, 60% baby alpaca, 10% cashmere, 10% camel, 15% silk.
THEFIBRECO.COM

Gridelin uses about 350 yards of Sonoma by Baah. DK weight, 100% superwash merino.
BAAHYARN.COM

Argent uses about 500 yards of Cloud by Anzula. Light fingering weight, 80% superwash merino, 10% cashmere, 10% nylon.
ANZULA.COM

Pavonated uses about 400 yards of Civility Sport by Elemental Affects. Sport weight, 70% merino, 30% silk.
ELEMENTALAFFECTS.COM

Infuscate uses about 650 yards of Selku by String Theory. Sport weight, 50% silk, 50% merino.
STRINGTHEORYYARN.COM

Ianthine uses about 400 yards of Oriana 8-ply by Space Cadet Creations. Fingering weight, 100% superwash merino.
SPACECADETCREATIONS.COM

Watchet uses about 325 yards of Fingering 55 by Claudia Hand Painted Yarns. Fingering weight, 55% silk, 45% merino.
CLAUDIACO.COM

Nacarat uses about 400 yards of Fourth of July by Briar Rose Fibers. Worsted weight, 100% merino.
BRIARROSEFIBERS.NET

Sinopia uses about 250 yards of Alpaca Silk by Blue Sky Alpacas. Sport weight, 50% alpaca, 50% silk.
BLUESKYALPACAS.COM

Filemot uses about 475 yards of Fine by Spud & Chloë. Fingering weight, 80% superwash wool, 20% silk.
SPUDANDCHLOE.COM

Icterine uses about 475 yards of Bugga, originally by Cephalopod Yarns, now by Verdant Gryphon. Sport weight, 70% superwash merino, 20% cashmere, 10% nylon.
CEPHALOPODYARNS.COM, VERDANTGRYPHON.COM

Fulvous uses about 350 yards of Bello Worsted by The Plucky Knitter. Worsted weight, 55% merino, 45% cashmere.
THEPLUCKYKNITTER.COM

Chlorochrous uses about 325 yards of Staccato and 80 yards of Silk Cloud, both by Shibui. Staccato, fingering weight, 70% superwash merino, 30% silk. Silk Cloud, lace weight, 60% kid mohair, 40% silk.
SHIBUIKINTS.COM

Other Works

So this book making thing? It turns out it's awfully addictive. It's only the first one that's hard! After that, it's ridiculously fun.

These are some of the books I've published so far. But I seem to have made something of a habit of this, so I can just about promise there will be more in the very near future

If you want to see what's in these books, or find out what else might have shown up recently, visit **PANTSVILLEPRESS.COM**. And of course, if you just want to see what I'm up to, swing by **VIOLENTLYDOMESTIC.COM** for news of all my latest adventures.

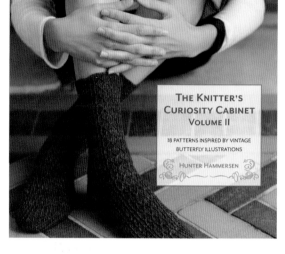

THE KNITTER'S CURIOSITY CABINET VOLUME II: 18 PATTERNS INSPIRED BY VINTAGE BUTTERFLY ILLUSTRATIONS

THE KNITTER'S CURIOSITY CABINET: 20 PATTERNS INSPIRED BY VINTAGE BOTANICAL ILLUSTRATIONS

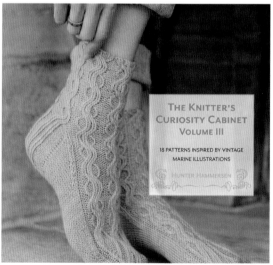

THE KNITTER'S CURIOSITY CABINET VOLUME III: 18 PATTERNS INSPIRED BY VINTAGE MARINE ILLUSTRATIONS